Unfolding Towards Love

Unfolding Towards Love

Martin Willitts Jr.

RESOURCE *Publications* • Eugene, Oregon

UNFOLDING TOWARDS LOVE

Copyright © 2019 Martin Willitts Jr. All rights reserved. Except for brief quotations in critical publications or reviews, no part of this book may be reproduced in any manner without prior written permission from the publisher. Write: Permissions, Wipf and Stock Publishers, 199 W. 8th Ave., Suite 3, Eugene, OR 97401.

Resource Publications
An Imprint of Wipf and Stock Publishers
199 W. 8th Ave., Suite 3
Eugene, OR 97401

www.wipfandstock.com

PAPERBACK ISBN: 978-1-5326-9528-5
HARDCOVER ISBN: 978-1-5326-9529-2
EBOOK ISBN: 978-1-5326-9530-8

Manufactured in the U.S.A. 08/13/19

Contents

I.

In the Beginning We Tumble into Light | 2
I Never Had to Look Far | 3
When Faith Passes | 4
The Boat | 5
The Census at Bethlehem | 6
Unburdening | 7
Love is Quick | 8
I Keep Trimming the Catalpa Tree Back | 9
Tender Music | 10
Only the Unbearable Silence Travels Here | 11
Psalm: The Horizon Narrowed | 12
This is Where Life Gets Interesting | 13
When We Are in the Moment | 14
Nothing Happening | 15
Walking in Love | 16
Love Pierces | 17
Swan | 18
The Spirit Moving the Silence | 19
The Quiet is Winnowing Us | 20
When We Meet | 21
A Tangle of Blueberry Stars is Breathing | 22
Lead Me | 24
Too Late to Make a Difference | 25

II.

April 17 | 28
Where Roads Darken During Daytime | 30
Requiem in Fall | 31
Unbounded | 33
Lamentations for a Natural World | 34

In the Fall | 35
Epistle about Love | 36
I Know What the Silence Is Like— | 37
On a Starry Night | 38
This is What Happens When Your Name is Called and You Missed Your Turn | 39
Destination | 40
What are You Waiting for? | 41
Love is Never Far from Us | 42
Blake and How He Received Visions | 43
Epistle on Healing | 45
Stations of the Cross | 46
This Is It | 48
During the Darkest Day | 49
Presence | 50

III.

Challenged | 52
Nothing Stays Here Long | 53
How Leaves Form | 55
Listening for the Voice that Seldom Speaks | 56
Sometimes, it is Necessary to Pull Back | 57
What the Soundlessness is Telling Us | 58
When the Heart Stops | 59
What Have We Been Doing? | 60
The Magpie | 61
Silence Has Its Own Language | 62
The Secret | 63
When it Comes to the End | 65
Unity | 66
It is Never Too Late | 67
The Heart Tells an Old Story | 68
Wakening | 69
All the Ingredients are Present | 70

When I Am with You | 71
I Have Always Known You | 72
Morning Light | 73
Where to Find Love | 74
Sway Back | 75

IV.

I Am Restless with Joy | 78
Hands | 79
Light Breaking Clouds | 80
Endings | 81
Psalm: All of My Life, You Have Stirred Inside Me | 82
Departure | 85
Daybreak | 87
Not Yet | 88
Light and Dark | 89
You Remind Me How the Silence Blends | 90
Finding the Blue Heron | 91
Playing the Pauses | 92
Like a Signal | 93
You Set Me into Fire | 94
The Soul Not Only Talks, It Sings | 95
We Never Love Completely | 96
There is Shining Over There | 97
Acceptance | 99

IV.

I Know Nothing If I Do Not Know Love | 102
Promise | 106
At Eternity's Gate | 107
At the Beginning | 109
The Uncovering | 110
What I Learned | 111

Is This Where You Expected to Be | 112
There is Nothing Insignificant in God's Eyes | 113
The Complete Stranger | 114
The Story of Our Creation | 115
The Midday Nap | 116
Recovery | 117
Waiting to Be Seen | 118
Entering Into | 119
Where to Find the Hidden | 121
How God Teaches Lessons | 122

Acknowledgments

I would like to acknowledge these publications in which the following poems first appeared:

Adelaide Literary Journal: "Love is Never Far from Us"

Atticusbooks.net: "Playing the Pauses"

Autumn Sky Poetry Daily: "April 17"

Bitterzoit Poetry Review: "This is It"

Blue Fifth Review: "The Midday Nap"

Braided Way: "The Boat," "It is Never Too Late"

Broadkill River Review: "Love is Quick"

Dash: "Hands"

Ecotheoearth: "The Quiet is Winnowing Us"

First Literary Review: "The Magpie"

Good Works Press: "Not Yet," "This is Where Life Gets Interesting"

Light: "Too Late to Make a Difference"

MockingHeart Review: "Destination," "Sway Back"

Night Garden Journal: "Sometimes, It Is Necessary to Pull Back"

Plainsong: "Waiting to Be Seen"

Plaza Jewish Community Chapel: "When the Heart Stops"

Poems for Ephesian: "Walking in Love"

Poetic Diversity: "Listening for the voice that Seldom Speaks"

Poetry Matters Project (Contest Finalist): "Daybreak,"

Poetrybay: "When It Comes to the End"

Poppy Road Review: "During the Darkest Day," "Nothing Happening," "Only the Unbearable Silence Travels Here"

Postcard Poems and Prose Magazine: "Is This Where You Expected to Be"

Progressive Politics: "Unburdening"

Red Wolf Journal: "At Eternity's Gate," "Departure," "How Leaves Form," "Lamentations for a Natural World," "Nothing Stays Here Long," "Swan," "When Roads Darken During Daytime"

Rhubarb: "There is Shining Over There"

Shelia-Nah-Gig: "Endings"

Sin Fronteras: "Wakening"

The Song is . . . : "Epistle on Healing"

Soul-Lit: "Morning Light," "Psalm: The Horizon Narrowed," "When Faith Passes"

Stone Canoe: "Acceptance"

Stray Branch: "What are You Waiting for?"

Sum Journal: "A Tangle of Blueberry Stars is Breathing"

These Fragile Lilacs: "Silence Has Its Own Language"

Turtle Island Quarterly: "I Keep Trimming the Catalpa Tree Back"

Verse-Virtual: "Light Breaking Clouds"

Wilderness House Literary Review: "This is What Happens When Your Name is Called and You Missed Your Turn"

"The Census at Bethlehem" will appear in a forthcoming anthology about Bruegel and Bosch

"Entering Into" appeared as a mini-chapbook (Origami Poetry Project, 2019)

"Finding the Blue Huron" appeared in the anthology, *Poised in Flight* (A Kind of Hurricane Press, 2013)

"In the Beginning We Tumble into Light," "You Set Me into Fire" appeared in the anthology, *Meditations on Divine Names* (Moonrise Press, 2012)

"On a Starry Night," appeared in the anthology, *Tranquility* (Kind of Hurricane Press, 2016)

"Unity," "What the Soundlessness is Telling Us," "When We Are in the Moment," "Where to Find Love," appeared in the chaplet, *When We Are in the Moment* (Origami Poetry Project, 2019)

I.

In the Beginning We Tumble into Light

In the beginning we tumble into Light.
We communicate in basic sounds
to express our needs. We need light,
sleep, and nourishment. Our frailness
makes tenderness and care possible.
Our imprint of wailing need is constant
and dependent. This is never forgotten,
yet outgrown. Our small reaching arms
and tracking eyes test what sounds
evoke and which are ignored.
Sound is foreign and learned, mimicked
and memorized, cause and effect passed
from child to parent, sharing common need.
From soundlessness to combining sounds,
making engagement, words are both archeology
and expansion. Communication is the beginning
of misunderstanding. We are embodied in language.

This is why it is so hard to talk with You.
Your words engaged my beginnings.
It should be easy as light and sound.
We should start with endlessly talking,
never running out of things to say or share,
or questioning, fishing for answers in shallow streams.
Let it always be this easy. It is easy
as finding secrets in an acorn among the wordlessness.

Silence is waiting to speak,
from the beginning, when all things were said.
I am on the ledge of awe.

I Never Had to Look Far

I searched the world for God—every valley,
every tree and low bush, every hill
and impregnable mountain,

every hint of water, even the lichen on rocks—
I looked everywhere,
beseeching, "Where are you?"

I spoke the language of urgency and emergence.
Nothing responded. Nothing stirred,
except my despair.

I went to where illumination was the brightest,
but when I reached there, it had moved like a question
not expecting an answer. God wasn't there.

I followed a music of birds into a crowded forest,
believing holiness resided there;
but God did not greet me or offer rest.

I glanced towards the universe,
the widest part of God's embrace,
requesting, "Are you there?"

I tried shouting, threatening, asking for signs
I doubted. I turned pages of sacred texts
looking for guidance, needing assurances.

When I reached bottom, I heard
"Here I am. Here I am." It kept rippling.
It went outwards and rescued my soul.

When Faith Passes

Either you feel it like a feather,
or you don't. Either it creases you,
or the air and your breath are empty.

Faith is bumping against your window
like a bird trying to enter,
not understanding what's blocking its way.

Faith is not ambiguous. Either you have it,
or you've never had it inside your toolbox
to fix what is wrong in your life.

Either faith is friends with your soul,
or it's leaping alongside you
trying to get your attention.

The Boat

When you see God as endless waves,
you will find yourself in a boat. After that,
either the world makes more or less sense.

If you find your hand on the till,
choose the way to go; if you let go,
the direction chooses you.

If you find yourself in large tidal waves,
you are in turmoil; if waves stand still,
you are stuck and directionless.

If you go without a sail, then you are doing
what is needed to be done. Who knows
where you will land? or when?

I see God's face on the water,
and it is not my reflection. When I look again,
I am not in a boat, I'm in a hand.

The Census at Bethlehem

> Also known as "*The Numbering of Bethlehem*",
> painted by Pieter Bruegel the Elder, 1566

We are counted, again and again
and again. We must tell about our past,
where we live, how long we lived here,
and not leave out any details.

How would they know we made a mistake,
forgot some history, avoided
some family disgrace? We understand
hidden threats when we hear them.

They come around again, asking,
challenging memory, clarifying
any discrepancies. Maybe we were found out.
Panic can appear on our faces, betraying us.

They come again. It is winter.
We are busy now with winter preparations,
we say, see the bustle on the streets?
Soldiers do not care. They have their orders.

I was in the crowd as a soldier posted the notice.
We must be accounted for; it is an order.
I could hear a donkey pass behind me.
I turned and saw a pregnant woman riding it.

A man led the donkey through the number of people.
I could see the determined look on his face.
I lost count of how many soldiers were asking questions.
All I could think was that they were not safe.

Uburdening

> Musician Daryl Davis convinced
> 22 Klan members to quit

There is a music to change.

Daryl Davis began a simple conversation,
in a bar, between sets of playing country music.
When you talk to a stranger,
you never know what to say.
Someone must start somewhere.
When Spirit leads you,
you never know where you will end up
and who you will meet along the way.

The stranger admitted in the half-light,
he'd never had a drink with a Black man.

Daryl simply wondered, "Why?"

When Spirit opens one door,
you never know what is on the other side.
The music inside might soften you.

Daryl never intended to convert anyone.
But, as they say, time heals all wounds.

Those men left not only their past behind,
but emerged into the music
of light and forgiveness.

Love is Quick

Love is quick-crashing meteorites.
We measure with all the wrong tools.

I opened a book; a stream of birds flew out.
Love is that startling, that unusual.

I've been trying to transcribe love's briskness.
I might as well toss words into the air.

I've been trying to catch love's cadence,
note by note into stanzas of music. Forget it.

Decades of bones have piled over the lack of love.
Van Gogh lost an ear over it.

Attila the Hun razed villages because no one told him
he was loved. The Fountain of Youth is love no one found.

The waterwheel of love keeps emptying;
all we have to do is taste it.

I Keep Trimming the Catalpa Tree Back

I keep trimming the catalpa tree back,
and when I'm not looking, someone snips
the top and ruins the area
where white flowers would have been.

The tree wants more light, less shade.
I want flowers, a place for birds to hide
and sing. Sometimes, there are compromises.
This is not one of them.

I do not want to mow the snowdrops.
I use excuses: they will die soon,
the winter grass is still flat and brown,
I'll get it done. This is not a compromise.

My wife asks with the most wonderful smile.
This is not a compromise. I rush about,
make neat rows of planted beans, cut some
slack in the mountain ash's heavy branches.

This is compromise. I promise. I want
more smiles. When she's not looking,
I stare at her; I stare when she's aware.
I'm trimming the way light enters.

Tender Music

I did not expect this sky to be talking,
although its blue lips were moving over the fields
like a woman asking permission.

Someone needs to listen. Someone
needs to bundle days
before they completely unravel.

Blue snow wavers, obliterating this world,
its trees, that river and its dragging
of debris like a silence of birds.

Someone needs to be tender music.
The world is waiting for us
to step into what we've never seen.

Only the Unbearable Silence Travels Here

Thousands of wildflowers have come
and gone, taking their colors with them.

A small thing, this untraceable silence,
allowing me to notice
what cannot be seen:

near the water-lined beech trees,
some pale purple-blue spring flowers
of the common hepatica,
emerge from rootstalks under leaves;

they only open a week or two—
such a narrow window of time.

They are already bending without wind,
timing to open at the onset of night,
listening for the movement of water
and light.

Psalm: The Horizon Narrowed

The horizon narrowed,
scaled-down to a manageable garden,
distilled into a single moment,
an unheard command.

There were no assurances.
Whatever would follow would be unexpected.

That is not what is important.
It is not the words we might speak next.
I promise you, none of that matters.

Even if our desire to know
wants to break free like a wild horse,
it won't matter—
an open mouth can pronounce suffering or love.

When I press my face to your cheek,
a groan is planted deeply within me.

I have bundled love like it was cut hay,
love pronouncing in me, and I've felt
all the separation merging,
all the searching ending.

A merger was not what I had expected.

This is Where Life Gets Interesting

I rise in this startled air,
an early song rising in pitch
trembling the furthest leaf.

In these bird-blast mornings,
I know what it is like to face each day
in trepidation *what will happen next.*
The days are approaching
like waves of returning geese
springing out of the horizon.

I will not be here someday to witness it.
Morning hymns will continue without me,
people will wake up at rise of light.

There is a male cardinal at my bird feeder.
I get to see it one more red day.

When We Are in the Moment

The world is fuzzy,
but you can step into it

and step out of it,
never belonging to either place.

In that moment, a clatter of silence
is immense. Light pours in open bowls,

mysteries leaving and entering,
rehearsing migrations.

Light finds its way, trying to decide
if we are worth having.

Nothing Happening

they say nothing happens
but early dew-light
shuddering low leaves

seasons are restless
like sparrow wings
whispering in flight

light flashes upwards
rubbing the deep sleep
from the sky

if left alone
the earth will return
to its natural state

intermingling larkspur
and daylights of sunflowers
their power to surprise

an outbreak of strewn leaves
try to escape
looping away

into the burgeoning last light
pretending to be streaking birds
and they say nothing ever happens

Walking in Love

What would you do to walk in Christ's steps?
So many confront us on the way.
Knock on doors until someone lets you in.

What would you give up?
Shed anger like a snake sheds its skin.
Whatever remains will be a new song.

How far would you travel?
No one will toss palm leaves
where you walk to cushion your feet.

Who would you not love?
Be a fisherman casting a net
to find new friends.

Are you ready to prostrate yourself?
It is hard to walk in love.

Love Pierces

With each piercing love,
we are never the same.

We cannot go back to what used to be.
We are never in the same light twice.

We wonder if we were that way once.
With each piercing, a heart mend—

a change of tides, a music of regret,
a séance where we can hear voices.

With each piercing, we're changed.
Not even our memories are the same.

We cannot ever have the same day.
We cannot always have what we want.

With each love-piercing, we fall in love;
free-falling, our hearts taking another risk.

Swan

In spite of its soundlessness,
the male trumpet swan chases the mallards,
making itself larger than the fear
flying out of the mallards' hearts.

The Spirit Moving the Silence

we discern by listening inside that movement
to hear what is not spoken
but felt

nothing seems to be there
then a presence seeps in

no one is there to whisper the words
although it resides as memory
of water and birth
a song that never ends

we are distracted when we hear it
suddenly a dark room has light

what do you hear

a sound less than ice forming
or a butterfly opening its wings

what do you hear

I see your head turning towards the words
going quiet
trying to focus on the source
and what it is saying

I hear that voice too
it is urging *listen*

listen

The Quiet is Winnowing Us

The quiet is winnowing what does not belong,
exposing the hidden so we can see it,
see it for what it is, its sacredness
within remembrance, an occasion to study

and learn, to praise, to seep into us, adding
to us, subtracting what is unnecessary, until
we have reached our essence, made clean, pared down
to a single lesson, almost declared we are holy.

But holiness is uncomfortable, almost fire
on our tongues, so we hold back. If we're lucky,
we observe, hold the quiet still, do not hurry
its message, absorb it wordlessly, be consoled,

center into that gasp and sigh, let assurance
please us, let nature nurture us, repair
our internal damage, release warmth
even on a chilly morning.
We release

like awakened birds into a gathering of trees,
until every part of us is disturbed, until there comes
another wave of release and another and more
that tell us deeply we're saved.

We are no longer sunk in remorse,
nothing is holding us back from being present,
and whatever remains is Presence,
the gladness calling and calling and responding.

When We Meet

I am coming to You
over a bridge of words,
not knowing what to expect,
not expecting anything, except surprise.

The table between us is the distance between trust
and allowing things to happen.
The music of questions plays in the background.

No one says it will be easy. Anything worth doing
takes work, takes time, takes often what we do not have.

I am opening the book of myself,
all the pages cascading out, empathically.

A Tangle of Blueberry Stars is Breathing

A tangle of blueberry stars is breathing—
fistfuls of dampening light.

Like an answer,
someone enters your room,
offers you a hug, and all the mean edges
fade, all stars seem closer,
almost touchable, all the words
you hear will almost heal you,

and everything will be alright.

Belief has strangeness—
we either believe in something we cannot prove;
or we believe there is nothing beyond us.

Assuredly, there are some grey areas,
but overall, these are the general categories
dividing us formally and informally.

We want a certainty that is never going to be there.

I rushed my hands and lips over my wife
to make sure she was real,

and the shape of her murmured
some words half-awake, half-asleep,
uncertain it was me, if I was real,

and we both knew peace.

*

This world is casual and simple,
yet words cannot say
what needs to be said. The world
is not waiting for me to describe it;

it keeps performing small miracles
and everyday occurrences,
as if nothing, nothing at all, is unusual
or disquieting about what the world does,

like it was all laid out beforehand,
pre-planned, and was waiting
for someone to take notice.
to say what needed to be said.

Lead Me

teach me how to enter a deeper silence
hover inside
reassure me
whatever is troubling me
will pass

there is so much to handle

I want all my problems
to launch off
like an armada of wintering geese
announcing their departure

I want to hear whatever is being said
within the silence
I want to harvest those words

teach me to how to stay quiet

let the words inside the silence
be lilac spray

Too Late to Make a Difference

In the jazz piano chords of rain
a glimmer of light is held short.

I was too late for the spiral of goldfinches
and the smoke that comes
off a hot pavement when rain first patters.

I am never at the right moment.

If the Spirit fell,
I'd like to believe I'd be there to catch it.
But I'd probably be elsewhere,

like this progression of rain
fighting the hope of light,
and not those raging circles of goldfinches
spinning color.

II.

April 17

It's April. It's snowing—again.
And, again, flowers close.

Snow is a cruel joke.

The world is speechless,
disappointed—
all this unfulfilled desire!
It is April, after all.
It's not supposed to be like this—

white, cold shock,
purpose driven away—

this peculiar weather,
this unevenness,
this lack of rapture.

It's our turn,
insist the purple crocuses.

Snow returns, anyway,
any way it can.

Death can happen at any time.

We can only sing our way forward.
The journey is long,
and the length varies
depending on each of us,

and when we get to the end,
tired, forlorn,
we will brighten up,
at last, and open
like spring flowers.

Where Roads Darken During Daytime

A house is near a grove of trees full of solitude.
A piano on the grained porch has somber notes.
Its sheet music can be weighed by absence.
Like a tree has confessions, a piano dampens
sadness with tiny mallets of spring rain.

Someday, the owner will return to the music
bringing the nearness of absence to each note.
The piano wants the melody of lovers
absorbing every fiber of their distance.

From wonder and resolution, every object is waiting.
Birds, dark as castanets, leap out of the cabinet of air
like whirling dervishes.

Requiem in Fall

*

Rain is bringing the fall season,
maple trees are dropping hints of loss,
memory shifts to other years. The world I knew
was never the same, yet feels familiar—
like I've done this before—
like practicing music scales.

It's colder than I remember. I blame this
observation on age. It kept raining yesterday.
Everything is second-hand.

The sameness is changing,
but You are not here to prevent it.

*

The maple is the first to let go and the first to return
a call-and-response song:
a season of transformations performed on a piano.

To say this is the way it's always been
is to ignore facts.

I've studied years of rainfall
and weather tells me
the climate is changing;

and You're not here to notice.
The rain plays its constant discord.

*

You're lucky you do not have to witness
the world failing. It'd break your heart.

All memory is nostalgia.
What I think I knew has faded in the past.

*

I've been quieted by other voices,
The unraveling of mysteries.
The altering seasons.
The silence in the garden.

I can only save this small space of land.

*

As light shortens into a sigh,
it is fall. The world needs repair
Seasons are crumbling.
Everything is quickening.
What is gathering is breaking apart.

You are not here to help me.

I keep singing what is sacred,
what needs to be lifted up
into memory where secrets and truth
are reassembled,

This is my song
coming back to the Source.

Unbounded

All plans are God's instructions
murmuring in our Soul, suggesting,
this is how to feel fully
and how to be engaged in this world.

This morning I listened to a bird
as it flew back and forth,
carrying pieces to construct a nest.
I never knew busyness had a sound.

The milk had a different taste,
and I had no words to suggest how
or why it was different. It tasted like Home.
It reminded me of belonging

and longing to be a part of the world,
to be God's hands making small miracles.
When I went upstairs, each creak asked,
What are you doing with your life?

I felt some part of life was missing,
but I couldn't name what it was.
What were God's intentions for me?
Why was I asking when I should be listening?

Finally, the answer arrived to me
when I saw a child flying a kite,
running as fast as his giggles.
I did not know how to enjoy my life.

I was too proper and set in my ways,
when all I had to do was relax
and allow wonder to overwhelm me.
And to laugh, like God laughs.

Lamentation for a Natural World

For years, the box elder has wrestled the wind,
the damp nights, the stars
grazing the meadows of the endless horizon,
the snow creeping up, the frost
speckled finger markings.

I wish I could say I could tolerate the winter,

but I have to go inside,
check the thermostat a couple of times,
wrap a comforter around my shoulders,
shiver out the deep chill.

The wind whines like a child
waking with night terrors.

I know the song of loneliness when I hear it.

That music settles in differently
than my body trying to generate heat.
Each recollection, each storage
of lost body heat, co-mingles like branches
in fierce wind, shuttering. Each star
is vaguely behind cold
meadows of clouds, snow sneaking in,
offering no comfort, no solace,
no rest from nightmares,
no matter how tightly I grip the blanket,
 no matter what song I sing to myself
to keep the sadness from entering me,
a deep and sullen chill.

In the Fall

I saw light
finding each leaf,
giving different energy:

some got quiet resolve;
others released their messages
only a few people could hear.

I heard: *Unburden yourself.*
So, I let everything go on without me,
breeze harmonized with the sparrows.

Unburdening myself, I never questioned
that healing, that gift of Spirit—
and then—I was everywhere

and nowhere. I listened to what was near
and far; my heart
flutter-spinning like a maple leaf wing.

Epistle about Love

Many are asking: who are You?

It is because they have not seen You,
they do not believe in You. Many see
but not with their eyes or hearts.

Because they do not hear You,
they do not listen.
They might not visit You
even if they knew where to find You.

When I first found You,
I was not even searching.
I had to opened myself to whatever happened,

and there You were.

Now I cannot stop talking about You.

I Know What Living in Silence Is Like—

imagine an estate of friendship being shared;
pretend that it is hands in absolute prayer;
think of it as speaking a different language
that moves quickly across the mute land
as quickening heartbeat shadows;
then see it sketching words of breath.

This is knowing our Creator
as more than an absentee landlord.
Just because we do not know of Him,
does not mean that He does not know us.

He sends morning songs to embrace us.

On a Starry Night

Van Gogh entered that quiet place—
the one where fireflies gathered
in communion. That one area
bounding with grasshoppers in his face
as Presence. He knew he was *there*
at the epicenter of released joy,
where the worrisome day and concerns
fragmented into powder
smaller than yellow pollen.

Above his brown straw hat,
galaxies spiraled as ballerinas—
such fearless Light—God turned his breath
into brushstrokes—Vincent felt his body
molding like bread dough,
weariness splattered out of him.

There was no edge between the horizon
and sky and God. He did not need windows
to see clearly anymore.

This is What Happens When Your Name is Called and You Missed Your Turn

God was thumbing through
the ledger of names
accidently touched mine

a sea came
into my second-floor room
luminous and melting the walls

there was a canoe of thorns
no paddles
but a written invitation

I never suspected this would happen
but in a world full of momentary seconds
I floated past the moon

I forgot to write down all I saw
it was like midday
when no one knows when it is here

the next I knew
I had circled back to my body
covered with spiraling universes

this all happened the same day
God created the idea of God
and someone else tried to take the idea away.

Destination

snow on the pine
is shaking loose found words

wolves flicker between the timberlines

there is no sound for miles
except where an icicle melts
freezes
melts
never completely releasing

listen for that stilled voice
speaking within us
breaking off like geese

when we finally reach our destination
we will dissemble into rain

What are You Waiting for?

we all have a vision of stillness

we believe it is tenderness
when deer vacate into air

let me tell you
none of this is true

silence does not need to explain absence

there are quiet lives within this cluttered world
all you have to do is listen carefully

there are mornings
when light makes its footprints
on the hard-wooden floors
as if to tell us
wake up

do not be disappointed if crickets wait
before making a statement

if you think this day has too much disturbance
then drench yourself in silence

Love is Never Far from Us

Love, perhaps, is not far from us,
yet it seems so far away;
we are overwhelmed with loss.

If we believe (for our belief is false)
love is gone forever, it betrays—
love, perhaps, is not far from us.

Love is never far away. Love is never lost.
It is with us every day.
We are overwhelmed with loss.

Small moments remind us what's false.
Love comes again, today and today.
Love, perhaps, is not far from us;

maybe, the sadness is just across.
We never know completely what to say,
we are overwhelmed with loss.

We try to hold on and let go at all costs.
Sometimes, love comes unexpectantly.
Love, perhaps, is not far from us—
we are overwhelmed with loss.

Blake and How He Received Visions

Blake was eight years old when he saw an angel
pruning in the rose garden. By the time he got his mother,
it was gone, but not gone—there was a breath of feathers,
white as snow or soot in the fireplace. *You are day-dreaming
like a troubadour,* she said, having better things to do.

However, once you have seen an angel, you are transformed.
You see angels pushing wheelbarrows of manure, or
hosting jib sails, or clopping on cobblestones
in search of sinners. One instructed him to write.

It was a commandment, really. He was not innocent anymore.
He heard their wings rustling like petticoats.
He saw misery around him and felt powerless to do anything:
a shadow of a lion, the color of a rose in flames, in London,
trailed after him, impossible to see if you are not looking.
Blake looked into its eyes like an angel looked at criminals
in the gallows with pity.

When something is interesting, it dies too suddenly—
scattering loose feathers.

He could try to put this all out of his mind. Pretend
it was a dream. It would have been easier.
Lying about this vision
would be denying the terrible beauty of it,
the essence of prayer would be lost.

He could not ignore what he thought he saw.
Dreams are something adults never understand.

He knew that angels laughed when no one looks.

In London, light was scarce, but here Light was,
drawing angels into his chest.

Epistle on Healing

We need a healing. As a nation we need a center
of reason. Instead, we have back-biting.
Some are ready to go back to the old ways, hanging
reason and sitting the body of logic on fire.
Some would act out, shoot their way
to get what they want, then ask questions later.
Some look for excuses to shoot without guilt.
Some fear they will be victimized, sleeping on a gun
as a pillow, ready to unload nightmares,
discovering later they've killed their own family member.

We need a calm that news does not allow us to know.
We need the thirst for better voices. Instead,
we have rationalization:
*they looked like they had guns; they looked
suspicious, out of place, foreign—
not like me in the least. I had to respond;
it might have been me; it might have been.*

If you ever felt a gunshot wound,
you would want all guns to be outlawed
as reasonable countries do.

Stations of the Cross

An argument can curl around a heart.
Anger takes longer to unwind or every songbird
goes silent. The quiet tells me this;
in this calm after that storm.
Some people grow stones for a heart,
some punt a resolution down the road.
Some swear they'll forgive
but find it harder than they expected.

I was doing the *Stations of the Cross*,
praying to give forgiveness,
but none of the statues told me how.
I was in the whispered hush,
wondering how Jesus did it—
forgive, that is—the taunting,
jeering crowds; the whips and thorns;

the wooden pegs—not nails
as we know them—hammered, centered
in the meaty flesh of his palm through
carpels, through to pain.

They nailed into the crossbeam, pulling him
horizontally with ropes, where he saw
multitudes shouting for his demise.
Whatever was done to me was nothing
in comparison, in retrospect.

Transgressions work that way. The agony
he must have felt was not my agony. Mine
was in a minor key. Yet, forgiveness
does not resolve so easily
as anger becomes lodged inside.

Jesus forgave a common thief
simply because that man had asked.

The thief knew he did not deserve forgiveness,
and begging for mercy was out of the question.
He simply suggested, "Remember me."

I tried to pray for the Southern group who beat me.
Forgive them? Why should I?
I stared at the replica of the Pietà
until I saw it bleeding. Anger hardens the heart;
it takes change to get to forgiveness.

I was only ten when they beat my dad and me
with clubs, iron batons, and brass knuckles
for being Freedom Riders going into 1960 Alabama.
They fire-bombed the bus while we were inside,
beat us when we tried to escape. Forgive them?

My dad did. He looked out at the crowd,
and saw beyond the loss in their faces.
I even heard him paraphrase, "Forgive them,
for they do not know what they're about to do."
They jailed Dad, then, and beat him in jail

I'm still missing teeth from then.
Forgive them? I hardly knew their names.
I had been on the dark side and back; knew it
for what it was. The statues offered cold comfort.
Kneeling in a sanctuary did not ease the pain.

By the time I was eleven, I had forgotten the pain.
Forgiveness had taken time
but found me open enough to offer it.

This Is It

This is the most they will ever have—
some wooden steps sagging in the middle
where people will always tread;
an old newsreel of their life. And this is it,
they realize, this is all there is to life,
whether it is paint chips blown loose
off the clapboards, or thin slivers of apple,
or that one moment when suddenness exits.

And this is it, all it will ever be, a disappointment.
Life is elliptical and strange to the touch.
This is it; it is not what they imagined—
vagueness and mystery.
And this is when they know
life's entire density is a sycamore leaf
plopping into the river as absence.

During the Darkest Day

Although winter solstice is upon me,
darkening every corner of my house,
there is always ambient light, a flicker,

a wavering of love, a greening of house plants,
a nub on a tree waiting to become a leaf,
a sparrow darning light through
to the feeder, a whimpering of snowflakes.

Presence

a sparrow landed on a branch,
barely moving the limb
with its light heartfelt song

this can be a quiet world
even when there is a song
moving in a tall tree

even if the melody hooks into my heart
this can be a quiet place
stirring from branch to fence to sky

this is such a quiet
quiet
world we live in

when the sparrow goes away
it takes its song with it
this world can be a silent place

III.

Challenged

All day, birds have been trying to fly
against the ferocious wind.
They insisted anyway,
on getting to somewhere
they needed to be.
They ended up going elsewhere.

Loss takes us to a place we don't want to be,
hidden far from us, but it was always there,
like those volunteer plants
growing from last year's flowers.

The unexpected is everywhere.
We just have to look.
This finding cannot be measured.
It's hard to identify
even if we endlessly watch for it.

Neither loss nor recovery is written indispensably
in the sky for any layperson to see.

There is no formula for how we handle loss,
no set amount time, no appropriate response.
Each of us has to find what to do.
Every situation being different,
having different impact and emphasis.

And the birds flew directly into the fierce wind.

Nothing Stays Here Long

The sky is heavy with grey clouds,
stacked like cords of wood.
A hand plow is stuck,
impossible to move.
Wind stiffens.
Long drops of rain streak like angleworms.
A clapboard house is silent,
oddly tilted,
dingy with chipped paint,

empty now —
haunted by yesterdays
moving further away
when the world fails.

A weathervane creaks in wind
without anywhere to go.

*

Even in blatant emptiness—
a flatness extending beyond sight
where perspective narrows into a zero—

even then,
even in the absence of houses
or trees or roads or hills or ragweed,
there is some life:

a fly; an ant piling dirt
into pyramids; a single anonymous bird
too high up to identify;
thunder full of electricity;
a car following a road without a name
or rural road number
not having anywhere to ask directions
and dust trailing behind—
otherwise lost,
memory burnt away.

How Leaves Form

at the tip of each branch
a green hope buds
a whisper

both stillness and

Presence

unfolding

a sluggish wintered soul
readying to appear
a sleeper

slowly stirring
when it opens from within
all secrets rush out
green words

Listening for the Voice that Seldom Speaks

She absorbed the immense tide of burgundy sunset
receding, an orange sun burning the center,
flaring out into the hemlock leaves
as a promise there will be more of this tomorrow.

She stood on a disappearing trail, waiting for a revelation
she expected to receive. But there was nothing—
no kind voice or soothing image or remorse
or fog rising due to the change in temperature.

She waited for clarification.
Then, she dejectedly went back through the spray
of white milkweed parachute-seeds,
these spiraling constellations.

She felt emptied for something that did not exist.
She heard it would be different—all who were seeking
would find what they had sought. But all she knew
was the silence; not the patience of waiting and listening.

All movement, all migration is a result of change—
whether bird flight when weather changes
or people fleeing war—seldom is this choice.
She couldn't wait any longer; she went over the rise.

Sometimes, it is Necessary to Pull Back

Sometimes, it is necessary to pull back
into ourselves—like receding tidal waves—
to find silence, settling into ourselves,
tension easing outwards, a rippling sunset
on water surface, to feel the air soften
its quiet brushstrokes.

I am sitting on a pier, looking at a lake
where the wind is not disturbing anyone.
The breeze is hardly present, but felt—
a baby's sleeping breath.

Across the way, by the shore,
trees are still. No birds flush among them.
The sun merges with the lake, slowly,
a descent of footsteps on carpeting of leaves.

We think we know what's important,
but we barely get past the surface.
We have so much more to learn.
Already, time is edging away.

What the Soundlessness is Telling Us

The absence of sound
creates the presence of amplified noises
so miniscule, we cannot hear them—

a baby sighs in an upstairs bedroom,
and a first-time parent rushes in
to check to make certain the baby is alright;

or a bat, glides after mosquitoes; or
maple sap surges into syrup; or chalk
scribbles on a blackboard.

Folding the laundry, I made the neat creases,
sighing a quiet memory into each piece,
the day after my first wife died.

When the Heart Stops

It is not anything that stopped; but me.
It was not this hearse of Death
slowing me down to find my Last Testament.

If I made the smallest dent, I hope it was with Love.
Nothing in this reflective silence is long enough.
Nothing stops ticking in order to speak of me.

I came into the world with nothing except Love,
and I leave behind nothing of value except Love.

What Have We Been Doing?

All summer, bees are transferring
their loads into heavenly oils.
What have we been doing?

All winter, trees plan new leaves.
The language of love billows on the sky.
What are we doing?

The horizon is rumpling with hills.
Whatever was crazy with business halted,
relaxed its breath to admire what is here.

What is taking us so long?
Go out. Explore what is provided.
There is some for you, some for me.

The Magpie

it finds broken objects
useful for spare parts to make a nest
for life to come

I feel no pain no uncertainty
if things were to stop brusquely
it would be alright
for I have built my own nest of left-over love

Silence Has Its Own Language

There are days when I am still ten, following grandfather
out the back door into the prayer of stars.

There are several ways to know silence—fishing forever
without a bite, your heart moving with a spring steam
defrosting;

or mucking the barn, rake scratching wooden floors and straw;
or cat swishing its tail before striking; or watching goldenrod
open.

Grandfather barely spoke all summer. No need to talk. Words
were wasted, when silent commands and nods worked well.

You can hear more if you listen intently—deer moving at dawn,
inventing silence; or the stilling of heart and hushing of breath.

More important, all of earth and stars and silence speak.
You can hear everything unsaid.

The Secret

Let me tell you a secret that's not really a secret:

in every pebble kicked by someone; every acorn
opening only during rain; every starfish
abandoned by a wave and rigid with death;
every mountain with its snowcaps, its raptor nest,
its small flower peeking out from snow
when sunlight finds it long enough;

every rasping wind; every drop of breath; every slow
almost-motionless turtle; every wolf caught
in a trap, gnawing its paw off to escape;
every deer standing in the middle of the road;

every ice crystal surrendering to melt; every
iris waiting for van Gogh to paint it again;
every stutter; every mill grinding, turned by wind;
every flute song; every verse of poetry; every
object, large and minuscule

is the body, face, murmur of God.

We do not need to believe in a creator
in order for us to be created. We do not need
to go to any church, temple, mosque, or field
to be a part of God's music. We do not have to attend
if any of those places make us uncomfortable.
We do not need to listen to sermons or messages
or understand the mysteries to be a part of the mystery.

We do not need to kneel, prostrate ourselves, or shake.
We do not need to pretend to believe,
or grind ourselves into salt to find belief—

all we have to do is be!

It's really that incredibly simple.

When It Comes to the End

When it comes to the end, it won't matter
if we are as rich as a sultan,
rolling in diamonds and rare rubies
or own a fleet of yachts
we never take out of harbor.

The only part that will matter will be
if we loved and were loved;
and we can't buy that—
can't own it, either.

Unity

Light and the Spirit was one and the same.
Darkness and Spirit was the other and the same.
Both were inhabited by a promise,
and a promise can be taken away.

Love promises a blossom in spring-melt,
a renewal of the hidden, still months away.

It is Never Too Late

A swan devours silence piece
by piece, quiet infinitesimally smaller,
as a presence of light
making a lullaby of waves.

The swan's impossible unfolding
for the living, for the days left to love,
is like telling someone how much we care.
It is never too late.

Even the sun descends,
light heaving its last breath,
gliding perfectly into death.
It is never too late.

The Heart Tells an Old Story

breathing is as easy as a spun silk spider web
holding gossamer light glinting in sudden
found light

no one can tell you it will be this easy

you have to discover this for yourself

Wakening

The intensity of love, suggested Wallace Stevens,
that is what is missing—*that* quickness! The *more,
more, more* we feel while in love. Birds cascading
like melodies! *That*, that is what is absent: the world
opening a book of infinite pages, fully felt. Our hopes
and barriers are the spine holding us together.
We never know what to expect, but we're willing
to risk it together. We waken to the sharp focus
of this world we never noticed before, and it is blindly
present, moving through this landscape.
We can almost touch the abstract shape of love.

Some people sigh for the lack of love;
some take for granted the presence of love;
some, the lucky ones, waken to gladness of love,
holding that quickening like liquid mercury,
like a bird trembling in their hands.

I left the bed with my wife still sleeping
bundled in blankets, the memory of her
from last night shifting through my spine;
I cover her again, kiss her exposed head, watch
her snuggle into the curve of love. I am fortunate
to know she was what was missing in my life,
intensely, yellow light everywhere, absolute and widening.

All the Ingredients are Present

All the ingredients are present: light, you, me,
black oaks filling out their promises.

Shapes become a small volume of houses
coming out of morning shadows.

Dogs stare at the last darkness, barking
it all away.

A person starts a car
rumbling like a man clearing his throat.

A woman is beating dirt out of a rug,
whacking like a lumberjack.

The best new is:
we are both still here to share this day.

When I Am with You

when I'm with You
a body of stars start to assemble

light removes sharp edges
off shadows
all love burrows deep

when I'm with You
I can lean off of a bridge rail
in full moonlight
water shuffles underneath
its unexpected reflection of love

a breeze lifts leaves to see what is hidden

every delicate
loving touch
finds us deliberately
love spills out its unbelievable song

as wonderful as this all is
love is pushed deeper inside
to make room for more love

it is incredible to realize this is true

I cannot speak about You without stammering
without truly being amazed

I Have Always Known You

You were here before the world began.
You saw me being written.

You were always floating like a lily on a pond
or the tree I took for granted.

I'm never certain if You hear me
among the thousands of other voices.

Some say we will meet someday;
how do I know that You are not already here?

When I open the curtains of day, my heart sings;
the sky cracks apart light—How can I deny?

Morning Light

Dawn: purple clouds dissolve,
noises churning awake. No one is out.
I am looking out a dark window.
The lessening of night has begun.
.

I hear the whispering of Presence.
Smallness unfolds.
Light is a horse plodding this way.
Its plow cracks the horizon open,

and seed tumbles in,
wanting to explore the soil, water,
and stirring light. It will be hours
before the sleepers' wake.

People will rise, face the moving sun
like sunflowers. None of this is immediate.
Everything worth knowing and seeing
lumbers by at its own sweet time.

Even a mountain or sequoia is still learning.
An iris is just opening its many blue eyes.
A woman is starting her early morning jog
after stretching in cracking light.

Light is arriving at the outskirts of a city,
edging its tentative way, neighing.

Where to Find Love

We ignore the silverweed
growing in ditches, its troublesome
silky-haired leaves and yellow flowers.
We've forgotten it's in the rose family.
We love it less than we should.
We forget the silverweed is a healing plant.
We should trust more
in what we can't see, can't touch.

This morning, I touched my wife
to know she is still with me.

Sway Back

sway back
in shouting dark-green leaves

move as gleaming birds

be the music of cranes
pretending to be clouds
before days of opportunities
have passed

the world is moving beyond us
as elusive as air in our hands

it is hard to keep up

I keep falling back
flailing at nothing
I can ever hold

at least I have you

the solid center of you
in the kitchen washing the dishes

soon you'll dry your hands
and walk into my room
as if you were light

what more do I need

let the yellow and spotted leaves
fall to the Nothingness
I will hold onto you as long as I can

let birds find dark trees
bringing light to them

I want the light surrounding your body
entering me

let cranes build nests
of stacked sticks like parapets

I know you will be here

IV.

I Am Restless with Joy

My heart is writing You into it.

I could not sleep—quivering
with anticipation—
I am restless with joy—

the sun moving its wings
of thrushes.

My trembling continues
with the possibility of more—
more garlands of light,

more burning-off dew, more seas
of Your welcoming.

My tongue
cannot express such exhalations.

In the wildness, in the calmness, in
the stirring bee hive, in the petunias
just beginning to rise, in the orchard
of hard apples, in the eyes of catfish,

love, when it enters, is not humble.
It wants to broadcast.
It wants to dance like a rooster.
I cannot hold anything back
when joy is escaping out of me.

Hands

Such unconditional hands!
They have held me and let me go,
and there was no regret on one decision
but tons of reluctance on the other.

Unforgettable hands of purpose!
Now they've forgotten and forgiven,
they've traveled to other concerns
as easily as turning over leaves.

Unmentionable hands! Too humble,
really, for their own good,
never bragging about what they can do
or undo. Hands of popular decisions!

Hands without any hesitations!
They have touched without complaints,
they have felt complaints in others.
Regardless, they sing praises of both.

Light Breaking Clouds

A dark cloud lowers
to the lake with precision,
forming a careful message,
breaking the ominous apart,
spilling light in haphazard directions—
some for you, some for me,
some for the grateful,
some for the ungrateful.

From the depths of despair,
we can only rise.

These few moments are all we are given—
this awesome responsibility
to share these small discoveries
before we forget them.

So, I rush out to tell you,
to shake you out of a slumber of not-seeing—
an iris sunset,
throbbing like an excited heart.

Light cracks out of us,
this way and that—some for strangers,
some for friends, some for the lost,
some for people finding their way into light.

Endings

In the poor light of late evening,
remembrance goes out.

Let it. Every day has an ending:
a lifetime of stars filling the sky.

Nightjars graze what remains of today,
making chinks in our heart.

Allow this day to end
with its needles of light piercing the dark.

Let multitudes of singing fill the end.
Let exaltations of the soul leap out.

Psalm: All of My Life, You Have Stirred Inside Me

All of my life, You have stirred inside me
and I waited for You—
    were You looking out for me,
    creating the peach sunset,
    amplifying each moment?

I kept waiting for a more complex statement,
but You were in the horizon, quietly unmaking.

    You were motionless
while the world moved all around You,
and You were devouring it all,
      simplifying each second.

    You were camouflaged.
You were this calm wind
    that did not want to disturb me.
You never needed to lift a hand to do anything—
    everything to You was as easy as breathing.

You were inside of me and I never felt your weight.
    How could I miss that fact?

   I know.

   I wasn't looking.

    And when I began to look for You,
there You were, inside of me,
      all along, a glacier of silence.

I had imagined Your voice differently.
    I wasn't listening carefully.

I thought I would recognize You,
      like magnets attract each other.
  I was embarrassingly wrong.

I never needed to look for You
    because You were always here,
        a typewriter composing me,
    waiting to see what will happen next.

Your voice fills the air like dogwood flowers,
    and I am a child, swinging Your arms
and singing.   My life is singing back to You.

      When you did not respond,
I thought I had dialed the wrong number,
or maybe I had been using the wrong melody.

      I waited for You
like an ocean waits for water to return.

    I kept plowing the soil to find You.

I kept building a nest, chirping like a sparrow.

      I had a premise:
I turned over the land, enriching the soil,
sooner or later, the land and myself
would be restored,
      and I would find You.

    What did I know about planting?

And then, the crickets came back,
bringing their chorus of enchanting music.
    They heated up the conversation.

I wanted to be restlessly found. I sent up flares,
    hoping You'd know where to find me.

    I became a song searching for myself.
        I wanted to see beyond—
        to see if anyone where there,
to see if my heart could be anymore elevated
        to reach the O*therness,*

to be in the alchemy of light blending into light.

    All departures circle away like gull's cries.
    One is either changed or unchanged by light.

I did not know You were inside me,
    light trying to break free.

I had to discover this for myself.

Departure

What seems like departure
is really a movement to another place:
whether to a city
or beyond the invisible horizon.
Will there be a better obtainment of light?

I have been on the move
like a nomad for a long time,
putting up temporary camps,
taking out stakes, rubbing my hands
barely on the surface — just enough
memory never adheres to them.
I know about disquieting places
in the head, in the body, in the toss
of dreams shaken loose from nowhere.

I have seen war
and how bodies can spool out while dying
like wrens. Their blood hangs like fruit
of wracked trees, yet still
countries are drawn into war
like it was a cesspool.

Today, a train pulled away
carrying people to their appointments
with tragedy. The heavy engine of grief
took a while to gain speed, then it left
behind schedule, trying to make up time
and distance. A person on the platform
waved goodbye, although the train
was further away than memory.

The passengers inside could see only ahead
where the future came near, then sped into the past.
The middle is always present and changing,
fixed and unhinged like wing beats.

Daybreak

I hear the distance calling
my name. I cannot avoid it
for long, but I keep it far away.

The distance knows my name,
but it's not my time to go;
a new day is about to break.

Here it comes as sure as it will go.
What have I left to give
that is still mine? Hear the calling?

Pang scatters far in the wind.
It is not that far away
that I can avoid it. Day breaks

and so too, does the heart.
Here it comes. I give what's left.
Was any of this really mine?

Distance beaks down into now,
and I say, *Not yet, I've got more to go*,
although the calling increases.

I cannot avoid it for long,
can't keep its distance from me,
any more than I control night or day.

Not Yet

All plants tremble in the fall sadness. Not yet.
Not yet. This way, that way, thrashing in gusts,
flinging loose leaves and petals, piece
by exotic-green changing piece. Not yet; please,
not yet. Rough tastes of wind pluck the plants apart,
making liver spots, rustic burnt sienna, yellow
jaundice, wrinkled. Not yet. No, not yet.
The fallen scuttle, settle, exhausted, then tremble
in strangling wind, calm down yet again.
Yet again, not yet. Every winter some might liquify.
Every snowfall, branches scold the season
for ravishing every leaf this way and that.

I know, I know, not yet. Yet we all end eventually.
We all head towards a home, this way, that,
trembling in sadness with exhausted breath,
not yet, not yet. I know my settling is coming,
spiraling downwards like leaves, that way, this,
and I am thrashing and loosening from this world
towards—not yet! Not yet, I am not falling, not yet.
I am not taken yet by the wind, this way, that way,
where seasons leaf by, pages of ravished endings.

Daybreak

I hear the distance calling
my name. I cannot avoid it
for long, but I keep it far away.

The distance knows my name,
but it's not my time to go;
a new day is about to break.

Here it comes as sure as it will go.
What have I left to give
that is still mine? Hear the calling?

Pang scatters far in the wind.
It is not that far away
that I can avoid it. Day breaks

and so too, does the heart.
Here it comes. I give what's left.
Was any of this really mine?

Distance beaks down into now,
and I say, *Not yet, I've got more to go*,
although the calling increases.

I cannot avoid it for long,
can't keep its distance from me,
any more than I control night or day.

Not Yet

All plants tremble in the fall sadness. Not yet.
Not yet. This way, that way, thrashing in gusts,
flinging loose leaves and petals, piece
by exotic-green changing piece. Not yet; please,
not yet. Rough tastes of wind pluck the plants apart,
making liver spots, rustic burnt sienna, yellow
jaundice, wrinkled. Not yet. No, not yet.
The fallen scuttle, settle, exhausted, then tremble
in strangling wind, calm down yet again.
Yet again, not yet. Every winter some might liquify.
Every snowfall, branches scold the season
for ravishing every leaf this way and that.

I know, I know, not yet. Yet we all end eventually.
We all head towards a home, this way, that,
trembling in sadness with exhausted breath,
not yet, not yet. I know my settling is coming,
spiraling downwards like leaves, that way, this,
and I am thrashing and loosening from this world
towards—not yet! Not yet, I am not falling, not yet.
I am not taken yet by the wind, this way, that way,
where seasons leaf by, pages of ravished endings.

Light and Dark

Whenever my mood dampens,
and I need the lift of larks, I recall
a morning, not so very far away,
coming at the shortest day of light,
through a blizzard and sub-zero weather.

I was shoveling like my life depended upon it,
not getting anywhere, more snow on the way.
Shivering, unable to feel my fingers, covering
my mouth again with a long handmade scarf.
I yanked down a knit cap to cover my ears.
What was that between the endless flakes
but the bluest half-light? Suddenly, I felt
I could do this. I could make it through this day.

Whenever my life lightens, finding joy
in simple moments, along comes a tragedy
to show me how fragile peace can be.
How easily broken and disturbed it can be—

then comes light again, and again I repair.
Larks swoop again.

You Remind Me How the Silence Blends

in this waterfall
white noise mixes with shade
from primroses
stirring the creek below
like an egg beater

when snow melts
it swells creek edges
threatening the roses

summer steams the creek
to a trickle of memory
in this absolute hush of water

its music is in the phrasing

those spaces between notes
and breath

in the octaves is light
mist
scattered into air

Finding the Great Blue Heron

The great blue heron invented stillness,
and practiced yoga on one leg with the cranes.

It wore a robe of white morning light.

It knew the patterns of fish;
the purpose of waiting to see
what happens next;
the patience of finding
what you need
and when to get it.

My wife bending her neck in blue reading light,
studies the same intense stillness
as if her life depended upon it.

Playing the Pauses

    A jazz term for the blank spaces within a solo

playing the pauses
the flexible give-and-take
of minuscule fluctuations in rhythm
that makes music "breathe" with life
is the same cadence my heart feels
when You call my name

there is that moment within moments
the same tempo of uncertainty
knowing you will miss me
if I respond to that other distant calling

you hold me in the music
jazz rift of notes fluttering
mourning doves
the breath within breath

Like a Signal

birds undulate until the sky
twists with them

mesmerizing
amplifying sound

noise turning
wheeling

unlocking and
locking in clusters like galaxies

birds connecting with our heartbeat
everything magnifying and moving

a signal
set into Newton motion of gravity

of every action causing a reaction
the swarm

a black fingerprint
dissembling on blue-paper sky

You Set Me into Fire

You set me into fire—Your words wash me—
You startle me into being—and when I think—
thoughtlessly, for I think less than I should,
that You are done, You are not. Stir me, settle me,
rustle my bedroom with your Presence.

Once You enter, forcing out is not considered
or possible or practical—prayers try storm.
I am combustible with Light—drenched by flame.
I cannot halt the morning from drowning in it,
nor would I try—it is not my place—nor desire,

trembling within and without, floors speaking—
O that You tell me! You instruct and birds are commanded,
rocks profess, the sky is flooded with intense love—
how could I not praise? How could I not be amazed by Love?
Ignite me, sink me, lift me! Do what You will,

for it is Your will—and what a will it is—obey,
I will, willingly I will, joyfully I am Yours—o breath,
o water of Light, o gracious You are and compelling.
How much Love can I give in return? For none is equal—
my secret heart is known and spoken, and spoken for—
I am so willing and so silent—and You are so precious!

The Soul Not Only Talks, It Sings

We all wait to merge back
into a singularity,
like punctuation marks
for the tremendous, endless silence.

I have been there.
And I have returned to tell you
the silence we hear
is unconditional love.

Wow, I could barely say, *wow;*
Where has this been all my life?
And I heard, *it's always been there—*
always—

ocean waves or light from the sun
since the beginning. I have always been
inside you.

I had doubted;
now I was being reinforced
by a voice reassuring me
what I needed to hear.

We Never Love Completely

We never love completely
without being hurt completely—
not even if all the world shifted axis
could we love enough—not deeply—
not even as love burnt as matches

could we love almost as much
as this hunger for love catches
in the light, when dawn is You—
entering like a bee into flowers do.
I shall never get so much love

as a leaf does, as the sun catcher does
having spent their lives chasing light.
We never love intensely,
more like a gatherer of air in a net
for time is never spent like it was meant—

something, something particularly
short of breath, distant as arms
not embracing what they should—
for I know this loss and finding, and gasp—
love is locked already in my past.

There is Shining Over There

    1.

I opened that door,
and it was the cover of an embossed book.

There was a clearer, spotless world over there.
All I had to cross the threshold,
to be in a field of angels, numerous as clover.
All I had to do was believe —
and my world would be a crystal chalice.
All I had to do was hear the pipe organ of my heart.
Nothing could be more understandable.

What stilled me? Why couldn't I just fall into it,
know it was gentle as goose down pillows?

There was an endless path.
There were fervent trees shouting to cross over.
Immeasurable cloaks of clouds parted their wings.
I could be immersed in water and never drown.
It felt like I had been there before.
It felt more like home than where I was.

I could hold all the stars to my chest, if I wanted to,
embracing all those unanswered prayers of children.

I gratefully entered.

2.

Things like this could happen to you.
What is holding you back?
Trust is always the first and last thing in life.
We must trust to continue to try
and if we fail, try again. We must trust
when things come to an end.
Everything that happens then
is based on trust or loss of trust.
Letting go is a part of trust.

Release into the infinite possibilities.
Relinquish these last requests.

Let them return as wintering birds.

What is endless is beginning.
What is easy is hard when you resist.

There is an invisible presence watching you.
What will you do differently?
A voice you cannot hear is telling you
what you should do.
Will you hear it?
If you deny it, it will not work.

If you find a key to yourself,
it is not too late.

There is shining over there.

Acceptance

The beige sky unfastened its huge cathedral window hinges—
then, concentrated light,
that lingering kind of light filling bones
with healing and lasting for weeks. It was so intense,
others could see the joy in my face.

Millions of egrets ascending together,
merged into the sky in rapturous light.
All I could do was be drowned in light
and sing from the hills and the fields.

My heart was enticed, like hummingbirds
drawn to a field of yellow Indian paintbrushes.

Light brought every object crumbling to its knees.

V.

I Know Nothing If I Do Not Know Love

> Based on C. S. Lewis and his relationship with his wife, Joy

    1.

He had gained what he did not expect—a love,
sprung out of a longing he did not know he had—
from the gift of giving and receiving,
waves entering and receding, a motion
as slow as a daffodil trying to decide whether
or not to challenge the changeable weather.

He was not searching for love. He felt too old for love,
too unwanted, too stacked with loneliness,
thinking prayer was more than enough.

Foolish, foolish man.

He was a man considered wise by many,
but God saw into his heart
that which he could not see,
blinded by his simple understanding
of God's commandment to him.
Foolish man,

foolish, foolish man. To think he knew
more than God what he needed to be
wholly whole, woven into a caring
that he stifled into a small pocket
and never looked at again, until,

until God sprung into his heart,
vibrant as yellow daffodils opening,
proclaiming, *Look! Look!*
Look foolish, foolish man!

And he never knew what had happened
until it transformed within him,
an uncoupling from loss into coupling
with love.
God stepped into him, crossing over
the threshold of his heart, declaring,
Look! You simple, lonely man;
allow Love to entangle you
with roots, deep through the soil
of your Soul.

He did not know how lonely he was
until he trembled before God's wisdom
and beheld his offering to him, Joy,

as she entered into his house, Joy,
humming in every room, Joy watering
daffodils, Joy humbling him to his knees,
bringing him to his senses, Joy cleaning
the empty rooms of his heart.

2.

Then, Joy was terminally sick.
He worried over Joy, praying for a cure,
but she belonged to God.
God needed Joy more than he did.
His faith became faithless,
his moaning shook the house,
rattling the books
in the crowded bookcases: "Why Joy?
Why not me?"

He began trying to reason with God,
offered myself in a trade,
thinking it was a bargain.
Foolish, foolish man.

He no sooner knew Joy
then Joy was being escorted away from him.

He began questioning God's infinite wisdom.
Foolish, foolish man.
Instead, his faith was being questioned.

And when Joy was taken, lingering
and suffering, he saw her fear
sweating on her forehead,
like angel tears.

He realized at that terrible moment,
it was his own fear he was seeing,
clouds having God's face,
reminding him of God's wisdom.

In his grief, he found absolution.
He finally understood God's plan
was not necessary his plan.
He was to learn Love,
experience Joy and sadness—
its finding and losing;
the inner workings of the heart,
and how it is a timepiece
that can stop at any moment.

Foolish, foolish, man—
God knew him better
than he knew himself.

He could read every book ever written,
memorize every passage
and recite each word in exact order,
but if he did not know Love,
how would he know about the human condition,
the weakness and strength
of the heart when in Love,
without knowing Joy?

Love raining like daffodil petals.
Love that is reborn,
again, and again.

Promise

I said, I'd follow You,
if I could find You,
if I didn't get lost, again,
along the way. I kept waiting
for a bush to burst into flame,
Your face lit and glowing.

The land bulges with mountains,
or dips into fields of endlessness.

I was searching for signs, omens,
clues among the shimmering water.

I couldn't follow You.

Then, I realized,
You were everywhere—

in every rock, tree, bird in flight,
the face of strangers,
the tiredness of migrants escaping war,
the soft tones of music
when the horizon is flowing with pink light.

I didn't have to go anywhere. You were here
and there and places I could not see.

You have been here all along.

I just wasn't listening.

At Eternity's Gate

> Based on the lithograph Van Gogh made
> in The Hague, 1882

He should have seen this coming,
this intense sorrow and searching for *That of God*

in every small thing, even in the coal mines
and wheat fields and among the dispossessed.

This deepness of sorrow, this smothering in pain
made this man so troubled he could not see his way out of it.

When we see what is front of us
and how we got to such a terrible place,

there is no turning back, no amount of confession
or repentance—every loss narrows in.

Vincent had failed preaching to anyone that listened
and all who refused to listen; and no one heard him

and his prophesies. His brushstrokes of misery
cover the canvas of life with the boldest of color.

Vincent preached in paint; no one heard the message:
That of God was missing; *That of God* needed finding.

Could we see Vincent sitting at Eternity's gate,
hands covering his face, sobbing black ink?

Could we see the gates barred and notice—
the stool, hard as misfortune? On, the gates were invisible,

except to that dangerous eye of the Visionary.
He became insane trying to make his vision understood.

We always judge harshly those with special insight;
and those with Inner Light are forced to hide it.

At the Beginning

There was a time, when the stars reached down
to lift us up—but those days of actual salvation
abandoned those who ignored the stars.
When told to go somewhere,
people went elsewhere.
Their wandering continued long after
the wanderlust flamed out.

Nothing that was made was made to last.
There was no language that included Others.
So, they left out strangers.
Nothing caught anyone's attention;
nothing that meant some kind of connection.

Which brings us to here. Not exactly
where we expected to be.
The world is still being created,
refined, re-imagined. All the busy activity
goes on with or without us, like dreams
other people have. We want to be a part,
and also, to be standing aside, observing,
feeling either important or unworthy.

This is when we go still,

overwhelmed with the lack of control
we have over outcomes. Everything we try
can find its own direction, even if
it's looping back into the way we were before.

I am telling you some message
without understanding, exactly,
what you will do with the information.

The Uncovering

I came to the county line,
not knowing it was there—
invisible, arbitrary, man-made,
an attempt to limit and identify,

something that belonged
and surveyed into belonging to someone else.
So those redwings were someone's,
the same as those oak leaves, that
dandelion puff ready to be taken
by an aimless wind, those clovers—
so that someone might say, "That's mine".

But it wasn't some place they could own.
Sooner or later, the area would pass on
to someone else, as easily as dandelion seeds.
Sooner or later, the land would come back to God.
Weeds would take over. Beetles would still crawl
unobtrusively, like signatures on the land.

We cannot expect any of this world to last,
but the land will outlast us.

Already, my name is being called,
and I'm ignoring it.
I'm digging my heels in. I am proclaiming,
"I'm not done; I'm just only beginning."

And I am passed-over.

What I Learned

I am stirring the dried leaves into dust
exposing the spring flowers.
The wind is yanking on my ski cap,
playfully, acknowledging, I'm not all that bad,
after all. *Maybe, later,* suggests the Presence,

Maybe later.

Perhaps, the Presence will wait.
Perhaps, not.

This is a picture of Belief
one could stretch
further than the universe.

Is This Where You Expected to Be

go among the asters and milkweed
if need be
to escape what you're fleeing from
until it is long behind you

mark it well
you can come back to it
you'll probably want this release
some dismal day
when the sky slouches
with partial rain

peace is hard to find
memorize where you found it
expect it to be as good as before

maybe even better

There is Nothing Insignificant in God's Eyes

it was less than one hair
on the donkey's back
that carried Jesus
bearing that awesome weight

it was less than the flea
told not to bite
until the journey was complete
not knowing
the journey would never be finished

it was less than one piece of dust
on Jesus's sandal

in spite of all that
the palm leaf was one of many
laid out
to soften that harsh journey
even if only for a moment

if only

if only

if only

The Complete Stranger

you cannot nail the spirit down
if it wants to move around

it does not want to return
empty-handed

it does not accept substitutes
it longs for attachment

it wants the silence
working in your heart

it wants to assemble music
from pebbles or sand

it wants certain clouds
and perceptions of moon-cast light

it does not want intermissions
it desires genuine apologies

it demands clarity and purpose
found entangled in forgiveness

you cannot stop the spirit
its persistence to belong

The Story of Our Creation

We are the Word translated into existence
from concentrated light passing through
mountains and water, words avalanching,

like unfinished love,
appearing among spring's purple crocuses.

We became flesh and blood
in the gradually dissolving transformation,
that chemical chain-reaction.

After such disbursement,
every moment following is less
than one pine needle
among thousands fallen in a forest.

We were made flesh with newness
and moments yet to come—

hiding in shadows
are all the tomorrows and goodbyes.

The comforting and frightening moon,
removed by cloud cover,
is feeling its way in the dark.

From here on in, it could only get worse
to the point we get exhausted with loss,
and recover, filling with light,
beginning again like a next chapter.

The Midday Nap

> Based on the painting, "*The Midday Nap*"
> by Vincent Van Gough, 1889

Not so fast, world. Not so fast. There is time
for things both pleasurable and work
so tiring, your arms are ropes of pain.

We need to find that moment when things rest
in a field of cut hay, under a triangle shade,
far from the fall harvest, far from exhaustion.

I have learned to take these short siestas,
while the sun plods like a horse never stopping.
A few minutes are all I need.

I am more with the shadows than not. I squint
under a straw hat into what needs to be done.
These are seasons of endless roped haystacks.

I shrug muscles already feeling the swinging scythe.
Already gone to where things are never interrupted.
Gone like peaches canned. Or fences mended and breaking.

What is held? The sky is yellow felled grains.
It always will be planted and harvest again.
Always will be this way. Always was.

There will always be couples resting in shade.
They will work until the day is bundled as the hay,
where love is always beginning and ending.

Recovery

there is a thin line between ecstasy
and heartbroken

a musical rhythm
to life and death

an arabesque of harmonics
trembling in the backyard

all questions are wasps
stirring loss

half-drawn eyes
find turned-down sheets

my wife cascades as laughter
gentle as paintbrushes tips

Waiting to Be Seen

Light hazed in morning,
uncertain what color to choose
or if to blend them all,

without understanding that
if you mix all the colors
they become muddy.

Things vanish in fog,
making near-accidents.
That is why the geese are low,

shredding the fog. That's why
we hear their waning cries
long after they're gone.

The world is straining to be seen.

Entering Into

    1.

the life I have lived
is nothing more or less
than vapor from my lungs
on a cold-still day

I am aching to be more
but I tend to be less

    2.

there is little time
to look ahead
into the transforming
light
to witness
the cumulative impact

all I can do
is prepare

    3.

heartsickness
is caused by absence
when it touches us

I search for the source
of water
to see if this is fresh
and taste
the chill of joy

    4.

the dreamer enters songs
like someone kissed
on cheeks
blushes

I enter the green waters
in filtered light

    5.

when you enter silence
like wind turning
a mill's blades
stirring shadows
you'll have both feet
deep in the stillness
churning with it

    6.

I've been reading the air
and accents of light
to find out what is being said

I'm listening
like low tide takes away
all loss
into the forever

Where to Find the Hidden

No matter how many disappointments
come knocking at my door, I find
a stray chicory in my garden,
hiding like a shy child; or a blue jay
warning about the feral cat; or a quick
rain-spurt darts by, hardly wetting the area.

It is never enough. I want the more-or-less,
as long as the world keeps ambling by.

God is hiding everywhere, in everything.
It is like opening a treasure chest,
discovering all the goodies before they're gone.

Even on this cold morning, God passes by,
and roses deconstruct petals for God's feet.
The sun has the scent of pink lilacs.
After it rains, a robin hopes worms get caught
on the drying pavement.

All of this is more than enough when eventually
every piece of love comes back.

How God Teaches Lessons

    1.

write down what you want to discuss
before you forget it
before a breath of wind is on your neck

or else its sound vanishes
and we can't remember
what we are supposed to do

    2.

snow-light
already forgotten
like a classroom lecture

the rhythm of our heart
is disrupted by remembrance

    3.

love is blown across great distances

anyone could snatch it
and I was ready
I got the good stuff

once I knew it was You
my synopsis fired
full cylinder
almost exploding

4.

we do not know why
longing tugs at us
trying to wrench us
into an out-of-body ecstasy

we know it
when we feel it

it's a homing device

5.

ever consider
ocean waves
music waves
waves of light
are all the same

calcium comes from the sun

we are starlight

ever consider these facts

6.

I found a remarkable garden light
unbearably so

all it wanted to talk about is love
all any of us wants is love

the sense of careless love
careening in our heart
singing hosannas

www.ingramcontent.com/pod-product-compliance
Lightning Source LLC
Chambersburg PA
CBHW070457090426
42735CB00012B/2583